Web Site Marketing Essentials

Straight Talk on Effective Design, Site Promotion, Easy E-Commerce, and More for Small Business Owners

Dan Stone, M.S.

www.DanStone.com

Copyright

For Alice.

Acknowledgments

Many of my clients have shared their online marketing struggles with me over the years, even if doing so was sometimes embarrassing for them. Their honesty has given me tremendous insight into how best to help other small business owners avoid online pitfalls and succeed on the Web.

Friends and colleagues have given me valuable editorial advice on this book and on publishing in general. I am grateful to them for their time, consideration, encouragement, and empathy.

Special thanks go to Alex Horovitz for his technical expertise and long-time friendship, and Elisabeth Osmeloski, Editor at Search Engine Watch, for her guidance, advice, and friendship.

TABLE OF CONTENTS

1

Introduction

Successful Web site marketing efforts drive potential customers to a site, succinctly communicate the value of the products or services offered, instill confidence in the visitor, and ideally convince him to take the next steps to become a bona fide customer. The small business owner needs to familiarize himself with a number of important e-marketing components. These include Web site construction, search engine visibility, and offline marketing materials – brochures, signs, and advertisements need to effectively refer people to the Web site. Since small business owners typically have modest financial resources available to dedicate to marketing efforts, it's essential that these expenditures produce results. Unfortunately, much of the money spent by small businesses in cyberspace goes down the not-so-virtual drain.

Who Is This "Web Guy"?

Many small business owners have made the mistake of assuming their "Web guy" is well versed in all necessary areas of e-marketing, only to discover down the road that their cash outlay did not yield the desired results, and their Web guy isn't replying to their e-mails.

In 10 years of working in the Web development world I have encountered only a handful of Web consultants with a firm grasp of both Web site building and online marketing fundamentals. Those with strong technical coding skills (HTML, JavaScript, etc.) often lack design and marketing expertise. Those with strong graphic design skills often combine WYSIWYG (What You See Is What You Get) Web page building software with a drug addict-like obsession with graphics, producing Web sites bloated with content that's not search engine-friendly. Small business owners don't need to know how to write HTML code or create graphics in Photoshop, but knowing enough to adequately supervise their Web guy makes for a wise consumer of Web site development services. The old adage *caveat emptor* (buyer beware) is certainly applicable in the age of new media.

Focus on the Fundamentals

What we're talking about here is a need to focus on the fundamentals of Web site marketing. Paying attention to the fundamentals of anything is rarely sexy, and in the case of online marketing, things can appear straightforward, making the basics easy to overlook. In Major League Baseball, for example, players seem to focus on hitting home runs rather than fielding ground balls and throwing out base runners. The high number of errant throws from the outfield to home plate – allowing runners to score – is the result of a lack of attention to the fundamentals. When professional athletes error they typically don't suffer financial hardship. Small businesses failing in their online marketing efforts, however, can suffer big time.

Return on Investment

Too many small business owners opt for the lowest cost approach when it comes to building a Web site. How many times have we heard someone say, "Yeah, my 15-year-old nephew built my Web site." or "The gal who designed my business cards did my site for 600 bucks"? Such an owner might initially be happy with his site, but 12- to 24 months later he'll realize what it may *not* be doing for him.

Crafting an e-marketing strategy is significantly more involved than putting a few pages online and calling it a Web site. That same small business owner would probably not hire his nephew to write his autobiography (albeit the nephew knows how to use Microsoft Word), nor would he have his graphic designer photograph his wedding, even though she owns a digital camera. So why would it make sense to put a novice behind the wheel of his Web site? It doesn't.

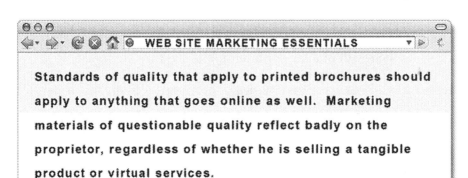

This book is intended to give small business owners with modest marketing budgets a look at the essentials of Web site development and marketing so that they can start to ask the right questions of their Web consultants, ensuring they'll get what they've paid for. This book can also be a valuable resource for the professional or part-time Web developer who wants to make sure his grasp of the fundamentals is firm.

This book is not a comprehensive manual on Web site development. Though it does cover a wide variety of topics, it is purposely more CliffsNotes than textbook, and more self-help than get help. Its primary aim is not intended to generate business for the author. Rather, the goal is to help other small business owners, who often don't have a full-time marketing person to rely on, grasp the fundamentals of online marketing to keep their Web guy, and their budget, in check.

2

Effective Site Design:
The Universal Home Page Formula

Around the time of the dot-com boom, the variety of site layouts and user interfaces one might encounter in an afternoon of Web surfing was mind-boggling. It seemed as if every Web site had been built in a vacuum. Navigating a site to find what you were looking for was often a waste of time. Mysterious plug-ins were required just to view annoying animations with obnoxious audio – never mind that you had to wait for pages to load over a dial-up connection.

Today, bandwidth is up, along with the quality and intuitiveness of Web site design. Many Web developers and site owners, however, still stumble when it comes to designing or redesigning their sites. They waste time starting from scratch, without a model to serve as a design guide. Reinventing the wheel might lead to a unique site, *but at what cost?* On the other hand, some sites are built in just a few hours using rigid, ready-made templates that allow a person with no HTML experience to simply enter in text, upload a few images, and voilà, Baby Web Site enters the world for a few hundred bucks plus $9.95 a month with little chance of long-term viability. The best approach, and one that is more cost-effective in the long run, lies between these extremes.

Benchmark Your Way to Success

The concept of benchmarking is defined by Wikipedia.org as the process of analyzing best practices, usually within one's own business sector. Benchmarking is prevalent within the automobile industry, for example, and has resulted in dozens of features in common among most brands of cars. Manufacturers are not copying each other outright. Instead, they are mimicking or drawing inspiration from each other. Benchmarking attractive designs and effective features of high-budget Web sites is a great strategy for small businesses with modest marketing means.

Design Convergence

When we analyze the home pages of the best Web sites, the process yields valuable insight into what makes these sites' designs successful. These sites have converged on a design scheme we will refer to as the Universal Home Page Formula (UHPF). This formula is the outcome of Web design innovation and the benchmarking that has accompanied it. The result is better site navigation and page layout, and strategies to cope with limited screen real estate and the short attention span of users with itchy, mouse-clicking fingers.

The formula is illustrated and discussed below:

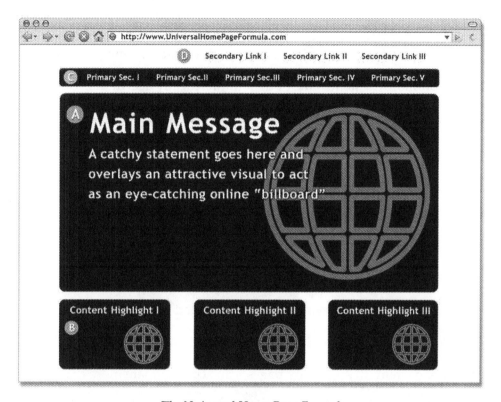

The Universal Home Page Formula

UHPF Web sites have a **Dominant Visual Area (indicated by "A" in the figure above)** that acts like a billboard next to a highway, its aim to grab a user's attention and hook him into exploring the home page and hopefully the rest of the Web site. A significant portion of the Web site development budget should be spent on this part of the home page, for the services of a professional photographer, graphic designer, or stock image purchase. As they say, there's only one chance to make a good first impression.

The formula also calls for **Content Highlight Buttons (B)**. Three to five buttons serve to focus the user's attention on key features of the Web site. These buttons combine text and a small image or background graphic to visually promote the item. One of the buttons ideally acts in the "call to action" role; it may be animated (e.g., images fading in and out) or have scrolling text of some sort. For example, an author's Web site may have a "Buy My Book" button, or a non-profit agency a "Make a Donation Now" button.

Less *Is* More

The content highlight buttons are typically located below the billboard, but can also overlay a portion of it or sit off to one side. Sites with a significant amount of content (that is, many pages) can accommodate more than a handful of content highlight buttons by varying button size and other visual characteristics. Most small business Web sites will benefit from a less-is-more approach.

Navigation is separated into two distinct areas. The **Primary Navigation Area (C)** is typically horizontal above the billboard and comprised of four to six sections – the major divisions of content on the Web site. Each section may simply be a link or, if the amount of content on the site merits it, a drop-down menu of links to the Web pages within that section. The

Secondary Navigation Area (D) is where links to standard pages common to most Web sites are placed. These may include links to the contact page, site map, site search feature, and home page (though links to the home page on the home page itself are not exactly useful). Since these items are Web site staples and less important than, for example, links to an online store or reservation form, separating them from the Primary Navigation Area helps those more important sections stand out.

Using fewer primary sections is wise for small business Web sites. This setup implies that the content has been organized hierarchically and the home page is not cluttered with links to every single page on the site. Once you give in to that urge, it sets a precedent: every additional page must have a link on the home page as well. Chaotic home pages are not a characteristic of effective Web sites.

The FordVehicles.com screen capture on the following page shows how the formula applies to one Web site. See the Appendix for more examples of successful UHPF sites.

UHPF Illustrated by FordVehicles.com

"Plain" Text Is Anything But

UHPF is more of a guide to home page layout rather than content, but it does suggest that key content (i.e., customer-creating content) should be prominently displayed on the home page. Many sites employing UHPF, including the Ford site and some shown in the Appendix, do not have sufficient plain text content on the home page. "Plain text" refers to text on a page that can be read by search engines (hint: it can be highlighted letter by letter with a mouse). Though these Web sites have text a person can typically read, text that is part of a graphic is not readily decipherable by search engines or the visually impaired.

Web sites with little or no plain text often make up for their search engine unfriendliness with generous advertising budgets. Small businesses that are not spending thousands of dollars on other forms of advertising (TV, radio, print ads) need to have plain text content on the home page to boost their search engine visibility. It's fine if this content is "below the fold" – that is, that it requires users to scroll down the page a bit to see it. Plain text content on the home page is primarily for search engine "robots" to pick up and use to index the site's contents, and it is displayed as part of the search results (see Chapter 3). No small business site should be without a paragraph or two of plain text on its home page.

Static vs. Sales Tool Web Sites

In general, there are two types of Web sites: the static, brochure type of site and the type that is much more interactive and serves as a sales tool. Which type of site should you have?

The brochure-style Web site is usually not much more than a static paper brochure transformed into Web pages. It gets the basics done and not much more. Rarely does a brochure-style site give a user a reason to return or refer a friend; as a result, its ability to generate sales and revenue for the site owner is limited. An effective sales-tool site is like a virtual sales person. It invites you in, gives you a tour, and includes valuable information and dynamic content that make you want to come back or e-mail the URL to a friend. To use a brick-and-mortar retail store analogy, a small business aspiring to have a sales-tool Web site needs a GAP greeter. GAP stores position at least one employee near the entrance of every store to greet customers and point out a special or two, the dressing rooms and the end of the check-out line. This practice is quite effective.

Give Your Web Site a "Greeter"

In the GAP analogy, the greeter acts like one or more of the Content Highlight Buttons (identified by "B" on both pages 15 and 18), highlighting "features" in the store, especially those likely to lead to purchases. Imagine if the greeter told every customer who walked in the door about every item for sale. It would be painful for customers, not to mention ineffective. Similarly, a Web site's home page should not draw attention to every page on the site. It's too much for the user to process and dilutes the importance of the site's key features. One exception to this rule would be linking to all the pages via drop-down menus used consistently for navigation throughout the Web site.

Formatting Other Pages on the Web Site

An effective home page will coax visitors to view the Web site's other pages. Navigating these internal Web pages should be straightforward and similar to the home page, with primary and secondary links visually separated. The home page billboard concept can still be employed, but internal pages should take more of a soft sell approach. The user has chosen to cross the home page threshold and take more time to learn about the goods or services offered. Shoppers at the GAP, for example, want their space once they enter and begin perusing the store. An effervescent greeter can be helpful, or at least amusing, but a hovering salesperson can drive shoppers right back out into the mall without making a purchase.

Internal pages need ample amounts of plain text content, supporting graphics, photos, and ideally, interactive features (see Chapter 7). Look for opportunities to add content. Two pages commonly found on Web sites, which can be great places to add content, are frequently asked questions (with answers) and customer testimonials.

Like the home page, internal Web pages should be visually appealing, but the emphasis should be on function rather than form. There has to be a call to action that's difficult to miss. It may simply be a phone number or link to a contact form, but users should never have to hunt for it. Special offers are great incentives for users to make first contact. Many small businesses send coupons with their quarterly e-newsletters, for example. Such offers should be stated clearly on the Web site in close proximity to the call to action: "Subscribe to our e-newsletter and receive a coupon for 20% off."

3

Search Engine Optimization Essentials

Google, Yahoo!, and other search engines are increasingly offering consumers new ways to find local businesses, to the dismay of printed directories like the Yellow Pages. Small businesses looking to prosper in the Web 2.0 world and beyond must build their Web sites for maximum visibility in such search engines' free listings. Search engine optimization (SEO) is the process of enhancing a Web site's content and structure to make it as easy to find as possible in the search engines. The SEO discussion presented below is meant to provide some essential insights when it comes to understanding this crucial component of online marketing. A wealth of information on SEO is available in bookstores and online at Web sites such as SearchEngineWatch.com.

How Search Engines Think

The goal of Google and other search engines is to help users find information on the Web by presenting them with a list of pertinent and valuable Web sites when they conduct searches. Search engines use complex algorithms to analyze Web sites' content and determine their relevance to search queries. The more relevant a site, the higher that site shows up in the search results (referred to as site ranking) and the more likely users will visit that Web site. SEO attempts to correlate a site's content to the most common "keywords" users type into search engines. Since search engines keep their algorithms under wraps (Google refers to its as the "Secret Sauce"), SEO consultants must study Web sites' content and rankings to infer how the algorithms work. Successful SEO efforts make Web sites more visible in the search engines, but do not generate online sales by themselves.

To better understand how search engines work, it helps to note that their algorithms are modeled after the academic research process (at least the way it was done pre-Web). A researcher begins a project by going to the library, intent on finding relevant journal articles and books. He might look through an index of all articles published on a subject and then locate those that seem promising. The articles will include bibliographies, and the more articles and bibliographies the researcher reviews, the more he may see a pattern emerge – the articles will likely cite the same few "parent" sources. For example, if looking into the poliovirus, the researcher would inevitably be led to papers by Dr. Jonas Salk, the scientist who developed the polio vaccine. Researching physics would lead to Einstein, psychology to Freud, etc.

Web sites ranked near the top of the search engine results for any given query are placed there, in part, because they are identified as parent sites and likely to be valuable sources of the information the user is seeking. A Web site earns "source status" over time by being linked to on other relevant Web sites. Search engines see a link from Site B to Site A as a form of endorsement of Site A by Site B. The more links to Site A, the more the search engines see that site as a valuable source. Because such sites are presented near the top of search results (they are ranked higher), it makes sense that getting links to your Web site from other Web sites is essential to maximize search engine visibility. This is confirmed by Google in its "Webmaster Guidelines" (www.Google.com/support/news_pub).

What Are Search Engines Searching For?

The content on a Web site is the most important way search engines' algorithms determine ranking. From an SEO perspective, content is the plain text on a Web site – not text that is embedded within graphics. When it comes to plain text content and search engines, more is better, but one can certainly get carried away. As a general rule, the best practice is to do what would likely be preferred from a user perspective and then enhance it for the search engines. After all, it's users who will become customers, not search engine robots.

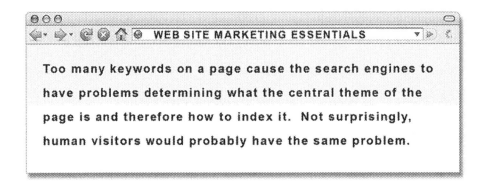

For example, a retail store specializing in gourmet cooking supplies might choose to have a single Web page listing all its products to attract search engines and improve its chances of being found when people search for anything ranging from "cappuccino cup" to "silicone muffin bakeware." However, it's better for each Web page to have a theme (like a thesis statement in a high school term paper) and to support that theme by using keywords in a focused, measured way, to increase the density of the keywords on the page without being absurd. Adding lots of pages to a site, each with its own content theme, and updating all pages on a regular basis, is the ideal.

If a keyword strategy incorporates the right keywords – the ones that are searched for most frequently – optimization should translate into increased site traffic and conceivably revenue (see discussion on keyword research, pages 31-32). SEO is a key component of online marketing, but it is not a means to an end. Similarly, the keyword strategy is only one part of SEO.

To better understand SEO it helps to begin with the end in mind and analyze what the search engines display in the search results.

Search Results

In most search engines, search terms appearing in the results are **bold**, as indicated by "A", "B" and "C" in the example on the next page, which shows sample results for a Google search for "virtual tours." If a search term happens to correspond to a portion of a domain name, that portion of the domain name will appear in bold, hopefully attracting the user's attention (this occurs twice in the URL lying just above the "C" in the sample results). Since the keywords "virtual tours" are part of the domain name "360VillageVirtualTours.com," that portion of the domain name shows up in bold. Bold is beautiful when it comes to helping listings stand out in the sea of search results.

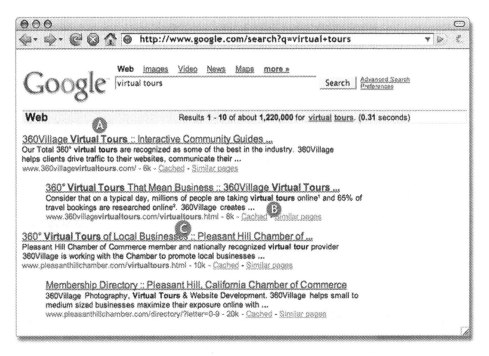

Sample Google Search Results

Since keywords will appear bold anywhere in the search results, including the Web site address, it's wise to register a domain name with keywords in it. Already have a domain name without any keywords in it? Have no fear! Chapter 4 provides two domain name strategies to increase the visibility of your Web site in the search results and aid your online marketing efforts.

Link Text and <TITLE> Tags

The underlined link on the first line of search results (appears in blue online, as indicated by "A" in the figure above) is what users first look at to decide if the site is worth visiting. The Web site owner controls the text that appears and becomes this crucial link. However, this text is often ignored by owners (and their Web guys), resulting in missed opportunities to improve a Web site's visibility within the search engine results.

If you look at the source code of any Web page, near the top is a section beginning with <TITLE> and ending with </TITLE> (in Internet Explorer or Firefox click "view source" or "page source" from the Page or View drop-down menus). The text between those "title tags" forms the link in the search results. Hence, it's vital the <TITLE> text contains keywords. Search engines limit the number of characters pulled from the <TITLE> text, so that the words can fit on one line. Packing a dozen keywords into the <TITLE> has little benefit for the site ranking, not only because of the character limit, but because search engineers are well aware of, and frown upon, "keyword stuffing." Users will be less attracted to those sites in the search results as well – they'd prefer to see a concise, readable description rather than a string of keywords.

The <TITLE> text should start with a keyword phrase and, in the case of small business Web sites attempting to attract local consumers, include a geographic identifier. Varying the <TITLE> text from Web page to Web page is also smart, not to mention helpful for users who bookmark multiple pages from a single Web site. Since bookmarks are stored by default with the <TITLE> text, if all pages have the same <TITLE> text then all the user's bookmarks for that one site will look identical, yet link to different Web pages – not too helpful.

<TITLE> Examples	
Typical	Dan Stone Photography – About Us
Better	Commercial Photography in San Francisco Bay Area – About Dan Stone Photography
Typical	Real Estate Realtor House Home Sales Seller Joe Smith …
Better	Berkeley, California Real Estate Agent Joe Smith Sells Executive Homes…

Other Components of Search Results

Beyond the <TITLE> text, the two other parts of search results are the two-line content snippet and the Web page address (indicated by "B" and "C" in the figure on page 28). The content snippet is extracted from the plain text on the Web page; the address, which usually appears in green, is simply the URL of the page as determined by the Web site developer. Site owners cannot control the snippet, but can control the Web page address.

Search terms appearing within the page address will appear in bold, as long as the address is not too long so as to get cut off. Therefore, a site owner will do well to ensure that pages are named using keywords (that is, save each HTML file so as to incorporate keywords in its filename).

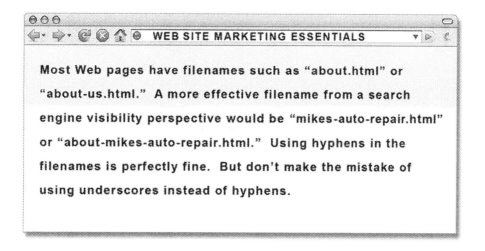

Choosing keyword phrases to use throughout a Web site does not have to be a guessing matter. The first step is to brainstorm, putting the obvious choices on the table. The next step is referred to as keyword research; it involves looking at databases of search queries to see what search engine users are actually searching for online. This reverse engineering approach can dramatically improve a site's visibility, especially compared to shooting in the dark when it comes to plain text content.

Ironically, some of the best places to gain access to free keyword databases are the paid advertising services. Google and Yahoo! both have keyword research tools intended for their pay-per-click advertising clients. Pay-per-click services give a Web site owner the ability to dramatically increase the exposure of his site. Those owners willing to pay more for each click their listing receives, move their listings to the top of the "Sponsored Listings" sections in the search results. In most cases, pay-per-click advertising is only effective when selling specialized products and services. Unless you plan carefully (ideally with the advice of an SEO consultant), you can spend a lot of money bringing users to a site only to see them exit quickly, without becoming customers.

For access to free keyword selection tools, as well as more information on pay-per-click advertising, visit the following sites:

- Google AdWords – AdWords.Google.com
- Yahoo! Search Marketing – SearchMarketing.Yahoo.com
- Search Engine Watch – SearchEngineWatch.com

Checking a Site's Search Engine Listing

Once a listing appears in the search engine results, the search engine's job is done – whether to click through to the Web site is up to the user (i.e., the potential customer). This fact is not as trivial as it might sound. The appearance of the listing in the search results, at least in terms of the portions the Web site owner can control, must be as attractive as possible to entice customers to click, to come to the Web site. A top listing in the search engines is only as valuable as the click-through rate it generates. Web site owners should be aware of how their listing looks when it appears in the search results. Checking how a site is listed in Google, for example, is as easy as typing its full URL (e.g., www.DomainName.com) into Google's search box. The search results will present that site at the top and the owner can review how it looks. In some cases, the listing may contain HTML code instead of the usual content snippet, due to errors made by the Web developer.

Enhancing Content for SEO Purposes

Once the Web site owner has completed his keyword research, he should ensure that there are at least two to three paragraphs of content (plain text) on every Web page that incorporate the keywords he wants to focus on. He should be careful to avoid abbreviations and use keywords liberally, even at the expense of repetition (but don't get crazy). This process often involves adding and reworking sentences multiple times to fine-tune their content.

Content Rewrite Example	
Before	Our PR firm offers services across a range of industries.
After	Our public relations firm offers public relations services across a range of industries. Technology clients of ours use our public relations services for product launches, trade shows ...

Site Navigation and Site Maps

Search engines analyze content by sending a robot to a Web site, typically its home page, and having it report back after crawling its way around the site via links. Most types of links can be crawled, but some types are more search-engine friendly than others. Some Web sites use buttons that change in appearance or reveal a menu of links when a user moves his mouse over it. Many Web developers are skilled at building these "mouseovers," but few realize the problems they can potentially create for robots. Consequently, search engines may miss entire sections of Web sites.

Web sites that use graphical buttons as their only form of site navigation are generally less search engine-friendly. They may have a text link or two within paragraphs, but use graphics-based navigation across the top of the page or down one side. Search engines need text links to help index the site, and an effective method of providing text links is a site map.

Site maps are like tables of contents for Web sites. They provide nongraphical text links to all pages on a site, giving search engines one-stop shopping for all of the Web site's content. An Enhanced Site Map consists of not only the links to all the pages on the site, but also short, one- to three-sentence, keyword-laden descriptions of each page. Enhanced site maps are like candy to search engine robots: small packages that unwrap quickly and leave them eager to come back for more. The sugar in the candy is the link text.

Link Text

A basic link on any Web page is composed of text; by default, it appears underlined and blue. The words that make up that link are referred to as link text. Search engines give significant weight to link text when it comes to determining site ranking.

Link text should contain multiple words (especially keywords), without getting too carried away. Since text links are typically the only colored and underlined text within a paragraph, they tend to stand out. The preponderance of text links on a site map, for example, is one of the reasons many users and search engine robots find site maps helpful.

```
WEB SITE MARKETING ESSENTIALS

Search engines use link text as a micro summary of page
content created by Web developers for the benefit of human
visitors. In other words, each text link has to give the user
a brief description of what they will find on a Web page
should they click the link to go visit it – like a little
advertisement for that page.
```

The worst possible link text is "Click Here." It contains no keywords, and users skimming a Web page have to stop and read the text around such a link (its link context) to figure out what the page linked to might be about. Using nondescriptive link text makes Web sites less user-friendly. Good Web design should make a user feel like a welcomed guest as much as it should maximize the site's visibility for the search engines.

Many Web site owners prefer graphical buttons instead of text links because graphically intensive sites can look more sophisticated. A good alternative is to have your Web guy use style settings to enhance the appearance of the text links so they're not quite so mundane. Style settings can give text links "hover" effects that modify how the link looks when the mouse passes over it – very cool, and search engine-friendly!

Internal and External Links

Two types of links exist: Internal Links take users to Web pages within the same Web site and External Links go from site to site. Both types of links are important for search engine visibility.

Internal links are obviously built and controlled by the Web site owner. As discussed above, keywords within internal link text are very important. Search engine engineers realize, however, that Web site owners can enhance their Web site's link text, so their algorithms are on the lookout for questionable practices that may attempt to tilt the search playing field off level. External links are a different matter. In most cases, the owner of Site A cannot build a link to his site on Site B without Site B's assistance. Site B's owner has to do it – and, in theory, he wouldn't do so unless he approved of Site A, to some extent.

Adding Links to a Site on Other Web Sites

Because external links play such an important part in search engine rankings, a species of Web site called "link farms" and another called "Web rings" sprouted like weeds during the dot-com boom. These sites exist solely to provide links to Web sites. They have no content, just links paid for (in most cases) by site owners. Online and e-mail ads for these services ran amok, claiming to dramatically boost search engine rankings for $29.95.

Similar services offered to submit sites to hundreds of search engines for a modest fee – all money down the drain.

If a Web site is not search engine optimized, with sufficient plain text content, quality link text, and an intuitive, user-friendly design, submitting it to a thousand search engines is moot. The site simply will not be found. That $29.95 could be better spent buying frothy drinks at an Internet cafe while formulating meaningful improvements to the Web site and finding other relevant sites on which to have links built.

The vast majority of searching is done using the following Web sites or sites that compile results from them. Most have free submission pages that can be filled out and submitted within a few minutes:

Search Engines' Submission Pages	
Google	http://www.google.com/addurl.html
Yahoo!	http://submit.search.yahoo.com
MSN	http://submitit.bcentral.com/msnsubmit.htm
AOL	http://dmoz.org/add.html
Ask.com	Not Available

The Local Search Phenomenon

The increasing number of users looking to find local businesses by combining keywords and geographic identifiers in their searches (zip codes, city names, etc.) has prompted Google and Yahoo! to create new features that fall under the heading "local search." Such tools combine targeted searches with interactive maps, making them quite useful. Users can start either by looking for a product or service within a geographic area, or by viewing all businesses surrounding a particular location, such as a major intersection – perfect if they're searching from an Internet-enabled mobile device like an iPhone.

It is extremely important for small business owners to submit their sites to, and maintain their listings with, Google Local and Yahoo! Local. Doing so is easy at these sites: http://local.google.com and http://local.yahoo.com.

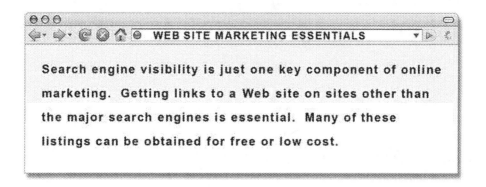

WEB SITE MARKETING ESSENTIALS

Search engine visibility is just one key component of online marketing. Getting links to a Web site on sites other than the major search engines is essential. Many of these listings can be obtained for free or low cost.

More Local Listing Opportunities

YellowPages.com is a popular non-search engine source for local business listings and a viable alternative to the printed version of the directory. A business can enhance its listing with a link to its Web site for as little as a dollar a day. In addition, many city government Web sites provide lists of local businesses (which may require a business license), and Chambers of Commerce typically have online membership directories with Web site links. Not only will search engines see these external links, but so will consumers looking to spend their dollars locally. As far as marketing expenditures go, these are great options for small businesses to get local online exposure.

Big firms with large Web sites and generous online marketing budgets have a definite advantage when it comes to SEO. Therefore, it is important for small business owners to make their marketing dollars count and avoid costly quick fixes that really are too good to be true. Over the long-run – which in "Internet time" isn't all that long at all – hiring an online marketing specialist can pay for itself.

Outdated and Shady SEO Practices

Many Web development professionals are behind the times when it comes to the best SEO practices. Therefore, it is crucial for small business owners to have some SEO knowledge of their own. Three outdated, but still popular, search engine tactics that are ineffective and could even get a site delisted from search engines are (a) "hidden" text, (b) "meta tags," and (c) "link farm" Web sites (refer to page 37).

"Hidden text" refers to the practice of including plain, search engine-readable content within the HTML code, so that it is invisible to human users. The practice of hiding text emerged to provide significant amounts of plain text to search engine robots while keeping page content clean and concise for users. There are at least two ways of going about this, and you can bet that search engineers are well aware of them. The first way is to set the text color to match (or closely match) the background color of the page. Small navy blue text on a navy blue or black background is impossible to see. This practice worked wonders in the early days of the Web, but the search engineers quickly caught on.

A newer method of hiding text is to move it off the page using style settings. This is easy to do and a bit more difficult (though not impossible) for the search engines to catch. The style settings can be used to position blocks of text left of the left-hand edge of the page using negative distance settings such as {position: absolute; left: -600px;}, which would move the text 600 pixels out. The Web browser software is happy to comply with these style settings, since it has no idea users cannot see such content. In the end, however, smart search engine robots render such efforts moot.

"Meta tags" appear only in the HTML code for Web pages and are not visible on the page itself. These tags store supplemental information about the site, such as creation date, author, page description, and keywords. Search engines used to rely on these last two, and Web developers quickly figured out that zealously stuffing them with keywords improved their sites' rankings. Today, most search engines ignore keyword and description meta tags. Small business owners should be wary if their Web guy thinks meta tags are an effective SEO strategy (he may also think a gallon of gas costs $1.50).

4

Selecting and Using Domain Names

When choosing a domain name, most business owners only worry about whether DesiredDomainName.com is already taken by somebody else. But the choice of a domain name can affect a Web site's ability to attract new customers. Users might be handicapped trying to remember a difficult one, and the choice includes search engine and offline marketing considerations as well. Therefore, being savvy about domain names is a Web site marketing essential, especially for the small business owner.

Domain Name Flavors

Domain names are one of the fundamental building blocks of the Web. They now come in many flavors, thanks to the more than 250 top-level domains. TLDs are the final portion or "extension" of a domain name, after the period. Over 60 million domains are currently registered using the ".com" TLD (the most common; about 75% of registrations), followed by ".net" and ".org" to name just three. Add to that a host of new TLDs for different kinds of entities (such as .mobi and .name) and a potpourri of international TLDs (.au for Australia and .vg for British Virgin Islands) and you begin to wonder, à la Shakespeare, What's in a domain name?

Search Engines and Domain Names

One question that often arises with domain names is, "Will my domain name help my search engine ranking?" The answer is an unqualified "possibly." The domain name by itself certainly does not play a huge role in ranking, but it is not irrelevant. It is definitely important when it comes to the user viewing the results displayed on the screen after running a search (refer back to the figure on page 28).

Using More Than One Domain Name

360Village strategically uses two domain names: 360Village.com and 360VillageVirtualTours.com. The former is directly associated with the company name, and the latter is strictly for search engine visibility – its primary use is online in links, and it is where the Web site actually resides. It is crucial that the two domain names both pull up the Web site, but that they don't pull up the Web site separately. The shorter version must redirect to the longer version for search engine compliance purposes. Search engines can penalize sites that exist separately under multiple domain names; they don't want those Web sites to appear in their indexes multiple times, as if stacking the deck.

Shorter domain names are used in print (letterhead, brochures, business cards, signs, and products) and can't be clicked and added to one's Favorites. The shorter the domain name, the bigger it can be printed on an item and the better chance it has of going from a potential customer's memory to his mouse.

Offline Domain Name Research Results ;-)

Two more examples of sites using redirects are Blue Kailua Vacation Rentals on Oahu, Hawaii (BlueKailua.com redirects visitors to Oahu.BlueKailuaVacationRentals.com) and blog.360village.com (serves as a shortcut to 360VillageVirtualTours.com/blog).

Using Domain Names for Special Occasions or Products

Many big companies use additional domain names for special marketing campaigns for a limited period of time. Given the low cost of registering a new domain and obtaining Web hosting services (aside from site building costs), this strategy can be effective for small businesses as well. Credit card companies, for example, frequently employ special Web sites during advertising campaigns. American Express launched a series of television commercials featuring celebrities describing their passions and hobbies.

The "My Life. My Card." ad campaign had its own Web site at

MyLifeMyCard.com.

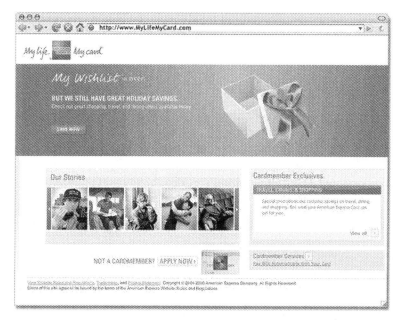

The American Express MyLifeMyCard.com Home Page

When the ad campaign ended, MyLifeMyCard.com was simply redirected

to the American Express Network Web site.

Below is a sampling of other special marketing Web sites and their owners:

- CampaignForRealBeauty.com — Dove
- FruitGuyFans.com — Fruit of the Loom
- LetsGoDog.com — Greyhound
- StayHGI.com — Hilton Garden Inn
- Priceless.com — Mastercard
- LetsGreenThisCity.com — Pacific Gas & Electric
- ItsTheMirrors.com — Texas Instruments

Landing Pages for Small Business Sites

Small businesses may not have the generous budgets of large companies for this type of advertising campaign in which an entirely separate Web site is constructed to go with the special domain name. In such cases, a good option is to configure the special domain name to redirect to a unique landing page on the existing Web site. A landing page is simply a page on a Web site other than the home page that serves as the starting point for a user entering the site. The domain WebSiteEssentialsBook.com, for example, could be set up to redirect and land the user on a particular page such as www.DanStone.com/book.html. Doing so requires only creating a new page on the existing DanStone.com Web site, which is much easier and less expensive than building a whole new site yet still capitalizes on the benefits the special domain name strategy offers.

Capitalization, Keywords, and Hyphens in Domain Names

When using more than one domain name, shorter versions are intended for printed, offline purposes, as discussed earlier in this chapter. When putting a domain name in writing, one easy way to enhance its readability is to capitalize the first letter of each word within the domain, as in PleasantHillChamber.com or CityofPleasantHill.org. This technique is crucial for longer domain names. Ideally the Web site owner has set up a shorter domain name for offline usage, but given the lack of available domain names, it's likely that a long and perhaps hyphenated domain is all that's available for registration. The capitalization technique breaks longer domain names into visual chunks, analogous to the way phone numbers are written, separating the area code, prefix, and last four digits.

Choose a domain name (or an additional domain) that has at least one keyword in it. If two brothers own an auto repair shop, for example, they should register a domain name like MikeandTonyAutoRepair.com in addition to MikeandTony.com. Ideally, the domain name should have a .com extension and no hyphens. Hyphenating a long domain can make it easier to read, but so does capitalizing the words within it.

The problem with hyphenation is that you have to say "hyphen" (or "dash") when telling someone your Web site address. "Check out my Web site at really hyphen long hyphen domain name dot biz," doesn't quite flow off the tongue. Users will likely have difficulty remembering the hyphens and where to put them when typing the address into their browser; such mistakes could even lead them to a competitor's Web site.

Web Sites Don't Sleep – Put Them on the Night Shift!

Assuming a potential customer wants information about a product or service at 11 o'clock at night, a Web site address will be far more valuable to them than a phone number and a voicemail message giving them store hours and location. Ideally, marketing materials shouldn't just list a domain name, they should invite and incentivize potential customers to visit the Web site.

Domain names appear on everything these days, from bumper stickers to wine corks. They are so commonplace that extra effort is now required to ensure they get noticed. Good Web sites become much more than static brochures taking up cyberspace. The best ones are dynamic sales tools – virtual salespeople. Salespeople, of course, need customers to sell to, and the domain name can help drive customers to the Web site. However, if one can't easily find the domain name, read it, or remember it, printing it on materials is a waste of ink. It's easy to improve the readability of domain names by keeping them short and using the capitalization technique mentioned above. The next step is to make it easy to find on a brochure, postcard, or sign. Don't be shy about making your domain name stand out!

Registering Domain Names

The granddaddy of domain registration services is Network Solutions, Inc., a reliable registrar with excellent telephone and online customer care. GoDaddy.com is now the leading domain name registrar, however, offering great customer care like Network Solutions, plus a dizzying array of Web site services. Both companies allow customers to conveniently manage their own products and services through a control panel.

Regardless of the registrar it's wise to purchase optional private registration. For about $10 a year, private registration hides your personal information from the public record, where spammers troll for e-mail addresses. It's also a good idea to register a domain name for at least five years. Not only is the annual price often less expensive with longer-term registrations, but fewer renewals reduces the possibility of your domain registration expiring, which could result in your domain being purchased

Home Page of GoDaddy.com

by a domain-scavenging firm. A domain expiration date should be treated like a lease expiration date on a storefront. A retailer would never be caught unaware of when his lease is up – a domain owner should be similarly on top of things.

So what's in a domain name? Quite a bit more than most Web site owners realize. Being domain name-savvy is prudent for anyone running a small business Web site; it can alleviate many a headache, virtual or otherwise.

○ ○ ○

← ▾ → ▾ ⟳ ⊗ ⌂ ⊚ **WEB SITE MARKETING ESSENTIALS** ▾ ▷ ⟲

Make your domain name part of your logo. If your logo is a graphic of some sort, perhaps with your company name incorporated into it, add some text in an easy to read typeface like Arial below it. Use the "www" part, capitalize the first letter of words within the domain name, and leave out the http:// That way your Web site address will always be easy to find, regardless of where your logo appears.

Notes

5

Blogging Is Beautiful

B logs represent a giant leap forward for small business owners, offering them a new way to add content to their Web sites themselves. Adding content on a regular basis is great for maximizing search engine visibility and keeping things fresh for users. That said, business blogging is not very well understood by small business owners. Those who are casually familiar with blogging might know it as a frivolous undertaking by teenagers on MySpace.com. Blogs written by "journalists" are more reputable, but their diary-like style might not lend itself to the business Web site. Or does it? In the July 2005 edition of *Information Week*, General Motors' Vice Chairman Bob Lutz said,

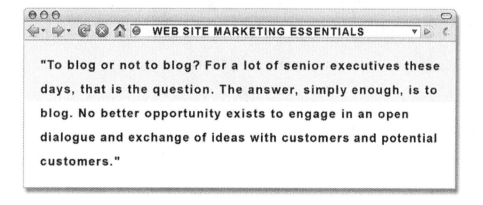

"To blog or not to blog? For a lot of senior executives these days, that is the question. The answer, simply enough, is to blog. No better opportunity exists to engage in an open dialogue and exchange of ideas with customers and potential customers."

Obviously General Motors is not a small business, but the effectiveness of corporate blogging certainly translates to small businesses that also want to communicate with their customers.

Wikipedia.org defines a blog as a Web site on which entries are made in journal style and displayed in a reverse chronological order. On a more fundamental level, however, a blog is a means for anyone with basic computer skills to add new content to a Web site in just minutes. If you can send an e-mail, you can create a blog. Even just a couple of entries a month can be beneficial for the small business owner. But what to blog and how to get started?

Free or Paid Blog Services

Starting a blog requires making a choice between free blogging and pay-to-blog services. Pay-to-blog services like TypePad.com give business owners the ability to integrate blogs into their own Web site rather than starting a blog at a separate address. In other words, the blog can be found online at YourOwnSite.com/blog, rather than at YourBlog.TheirBlogSite.com. Since a Web site's search engine ranking is tied to its domain name, incorporating the blog into your own site is a wise move. Free blogging sites, such as Blogger.com, do not typically allow a blog to exist under a custom domain name, but since they are free, these sites represent a great opportunity for

the small business owner to get started blogging.

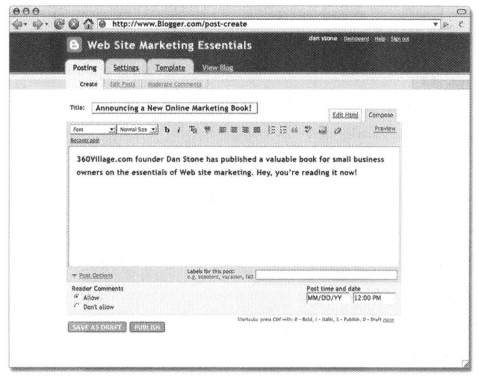

Blogger.com New Blog Entry Template

Blog Topics

The second decision that confronts the budding blogger is what to blog

about? Given that most small business owners are passionate about their

work and love to talk about what they do, it's somewhat ironic that many

find it difficult to generate blog entries. A blog is a discussion between the blogger and his audience, which in the case of a small business' blog is its customer base.

A successful small business blog will do at least three things: (a) make readers aware of new information, products and services related to the blogger's business; (b) keep the content fresh to encourage readers and search engine robots to return on a regular basis; and (c) enhance the site's effectiveness as a sales tool.

This last one is key. Why have a Web site for a business if it doesn't do its best to promote and sell the products and services the business offers? Since it can be costly to hire a Web developer to make changes and additions to a Web site, and since the products offered by many small businesses change frequently (i.e., retail stores' sale items and real estate agents' listings), a blog's ability to let the site owner quickly and easily update content is valuable, not to mention convenient.

For more ideas, check out the 360Village blog at http://blog.360Village.com as well as the sample blog entry topics on the following page.

Type of Blog	Sample Blog Entry Topics
Accountant	i. Tax law changes ii. Deduction Tips iii. Client case studies
Bed & Breakfast Inn	i. Special package rates ii. Local events iii. Menu updates and recipes
Chamber of Commerce	i. New member announcements ii. Local business events/openings iii. Referrals to new online resources
Chiropractor	i. Stretching at work tips ii. Recognizing signs of sciatica iii. Product recommendations
Day Spa	i. New products ii. Special treatment packages iii. Summary of health news story
Real Estate Agent	i. Property listings ii. Community events iii. Referrals to local professionals
Restaurant	i. New menu specials ii. Catering event descriptions iii. Online store specials
Retail Store	i. New products ii. Store specials/sales iii. Referrals to online resources

Notes

6

Making Money Online: E-Commerce Made Easy

Engaging in e-commerce does not necessarily mean a Web site has a virtual shopping cart and sells products directly to the consumer. A range of opportunities exists to make money online without a direct interface with the consumer. Small businesses that do wish to sell directly online can do so far more easily than they used to, thanks to competition and innovation between third-party payment processors. You don't even have to have a Web site to engage in e-commerce.

Selling Made Simple with PayPal

The largest third-party payment processor online is PayPal, an eBay company (PayPal.com). If you have a Web site and you want to get started selling products online quickly, it's a great choice. Your customers pay PayPal and PayPal, in turn, pays you. You'll need to set up a PayPal account ahead of time and go through some painless verification steps, but once that is done, e-commerce is only a matter of deciding what to sell. PayPal enables a merchant to sell a single item via a "Buy Now" button or multiple items via a simplified shopping cart. Either option requires only that you login to your PayPal account and enter item information into a

basic form (see figure below), including a description and price.

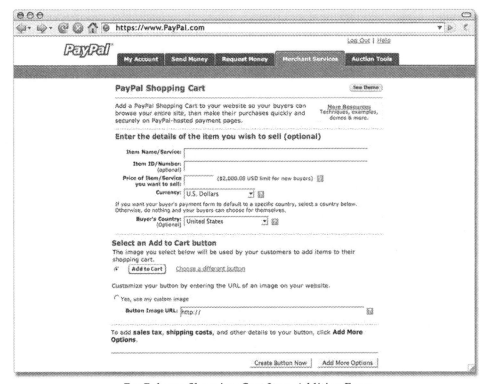

PayPal.com Shopping Cart Item Addition Form

PayPal then generates the necessary HTML code on the spot, ready to be

cut and pasted onto the Web site. The code contains a merchant identifier,

so that the proper account is credited upon each sale. When a purchase is

made, the customer receives a receipt and the merchant receives a copy of

the order, both via e-mail. Payment is deposited into the merchant's PayPal

account for withdrawal via electronic transfer or paper check when desired.

For the small business owner looking to sell a limited number of items, PayPal is arguably the easiest way to dip a toe into the e-commerce pool. There are no monthly fees, only charges per transaction – no sales means no fees. Three examples of live, simple PayPal shopping carts on small business Web sites can be found online at KellyAnnsDaySpa.com (gift certificates), KonaCoffeeBedBreakfast.com (fresh Kona coffee beans), and PleasantHillChamber.com (membership renewals).

Many online services offer full-fledged e-commerce capabilities for small business Web sites with greater needs, including GoDaddy (GoDaddy.com), Monster Commerce (MonsterCommerce.com), and Yahoo! Small Business (SmallBusiness.Yahoo.com/ecommerce).

Selling Other People's Products

Customizing other people's products is another great way to get started in e-commerce, with or without a Web site. Sites such as CafePress.com create virtual stores in which merchants can sell their own designs imprinted on items CafePress supplies, ranging from coffee mugs to T-shirts. CafePress handles both the e-commerce "back end" and order fulfillment, so the experience could not be easier for the small business owner. Just open a CafePress account, upload your artwork, and choose the items you want it imprinted on, and the virtual store doors are ready to open.

CafePress.com Home Page

Affiliate Programs

For service-oriented businesses that have a tough time coming up with anything to sell, there are dozens of affiliate marketing programs, through which you can make a commission selling other merchants' items. Amazon.com has one of the oldest affiliate programs; it offers up to 8.5% in referral fees, paid quarterly. After signing up for the program, an Amazon affiliate chooses which items available on Amazon it would like to sell. Amazon then generates special links for the affiliate's Web site. When a user clicks on the links and eventually purchases the item through Amazon.com, the links identify the affiliate as the source.

Other online affiliate programs include Apple's iTunes Store (www.Apple.com/itunes/affiliates), the Container Store online (www.theContainerStore.com), eLoan.com (www.eLoan.com), GoDaddy.com (www.GoDaddy.com), Wyndham Hotels (www.Wyndham.com), Nolo.com (www.Nolo.com/affiliate), and Vonage (www.Vonage.com/affilliates).

Notes

7

Engaging Users with Interactive Features

The better sales-tool Web sites use interactive features. Small business owners can choose from a number of such features that are cost-effective, create interest, and generate more traffic to the site.

Photography-Based Features

An online photo gallery or slideshow composed of professionally shot images is relatively easy to implement. Providing thumbnail versions of each image allows the user to navigate through the gallery at his own pace in whatever order he prefers (see figure next page). A number of software applications are available to automate the photo gallery building process. Google and Yahoo! have photo sharing services called Picasa and Flickr, respectively, which require minimal coding to integrate a photo gallery into any Web site, including blogs.

A slightly more elaborate, but still cost-effective presentation, combines still photos to create a video, referred to as a slideshow video. Software applications to create such videos are inexpensive and fairly easy to use. Apple's iMovie software comes free with new Macs or is available as part of the iLife software bundle for less than $100. Windows users can choose from a variety of applications by searching for "slideshow video" at

Download.com.

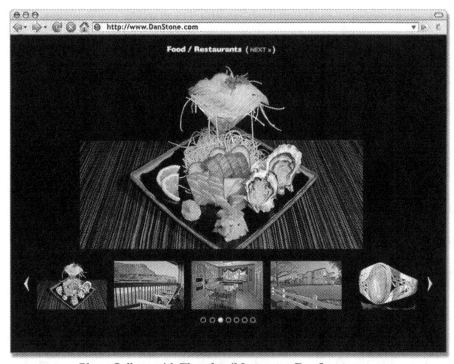

Photo Gallery with Thumbnail Images at DanStone.com

You can set the photos in a slideshow video to fade in and out with an

audio accompaniment, or voiceover narration (describing products and

services) for more interest. For a professional look, you can give the

otherwise still photos the appearance of motion using the "Ken Burns

effect," which is included with iMovie and other applications.

Virtual Tours

Another photography-based interactive solution for small businesses is the virtual tour. Virtual tours typically consist of 360° panoramic (or "omniramic") images that allow the user to move around the image – look up and down, pan left and right, and zoom in and out. Since the user controls the virtual tour, he doesn't just watch it, he experiences it, which is how any effective interactive online feature should work.

Virtual tours are an outstanding means for retailers, restaurateurs, and real estate agents to showcase their stores, restaurants, and listings. On any given day, more than two million users take virtual tours of everything from hotels to museums, shops to cities. On Realtor.com, the largest Web site for real estate listings in the US, homes with virtual tours receive nearly 40% more views than those without. It's no wonder users are quickly coming to expect virtual tours when they visit the Web sites of brick-and-mortar businesses.

As with any photography or Web development project, the business owner needs to make sure the end result will look professional. Virtual tours can have graphic user interfaces that include interactive maps, audio, still photos and other media. However, just because an image is 360° and interactive doesn't mean it is high quality from a photographic perspective.

Virtual tours built with 360° QuickTime VR images (Apple.com/quicktime) can be viewed right on the desktop or sent via e-mail without the need to go online. Ideally, the photos, virtual tour or slideshow video project should include online implementation in the cost so the Web site owner does not incur additional expense getting it up online.

You can view samples of all three types of interactive features at the Web sites of new media providers, including 360Village.com.

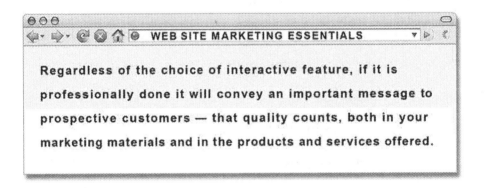

Regardless of the choice of interactive feature, if it is professionally done it will convey an important message to prospective customers — that quality counts, both in your marketing materials and in the products and services offered.

Using Flash

Web developers can use a program called Flash from Adobe Systems (www.adobe.com/products/flash) to create and play a wide variety of multimedia files (and to view video clips on popular sites like YouTube.com). Flash presentations can be extremely effective, but they can also be costly to develop. Any Flash file placed online requires users to have the free Flash Player installed on their systems to view it. Statistics show that most users do have Flash installed, but that's still not everyone. If you have a choice between a Flash-based presentation and a more universal HTML version, make sure you carefully weigh the benefits and costs of each option.

One basic use for Flash is multi-image animations in which one image fades into another. Flash handles this effect smoothly, gives the animation a professional look, and yields a small file (meaning it's faster for the user to download and enjoy). Other means of creating animations that predate Flash (such as animated GIF images) can still work well and do not require plug-ins.

A great use of Flash is for tutorials, or tours, that showcase products or services, often with motion graphics and audio. These Flash tours typically launch in a pop-up window and walk a user through a company's offerings. Users without Flash can still navigate the rest of the Web site; they simply won't see the presentation. Search engines may ignore Flash content, but it is intended for human ears and eyeballs anyway. These Flash tours are great for product launches, new or complex services that need more explanation than a static text block can provide, and any presentation that could benefit from a little interactive punch.

Flash can be used to create an entire Web site, from layout to navigation, scrolling content to dynamic images. Small business owners with big enough online marketing budgets can easily be seduced by Flash. Professionally produced Flash sites often look great, but just as frequently they're search engine-*un*friendly.

Three good examples of Flash tours are those for Google Analytics (http://services.google.com/analytics/tour/index_en-US.html), Yahoo! Go (http://mobile.yahoo.com/go/tour) and AT&T Wireless Push-to-Talk (http://www.wireless.att.com/learn/swf/push_to_Talk/business.html). Dozens of other Flash tours can be found by searching for "Flash product tour."

Using Digital Video

YouTube has sparked a revolution in video uploading by novice users. Given the cost of hiring a professional videographer vis-à-vis the benefits of interactive features, small business owners with tight budgets may opt for a do-it-yourself (DIY) approach to digital video. Good advice on shooting digital video is available on sites such as YouTube (http://youtube.com/t/video_toolbox) and other video-related Web sites. You can add video to your Web site by first uploading the video file to a YouTube account and then inserting a piece of HTML code into the relevant

Web page. Of course, the ease of this process is also what leads to the plethora of poor-quality DIY video online. In the end, hiring a professional videographer is probably worth it.

Turning Presentations into Videos

PowerPoint is the popular presentation software from Microsoft used in conference rooms and classrooms around the world. A basic PowerPoint presentation is easy to build and can be saved in HTML format or converted into Flash with third-party software for posting online. Apple's presentation software, called Keynote, has even more advanced features and cinema-quality animation capabilities. With Keynote, you can add a voiceover to the presentation then save it as a self-playing QuickTime movie. This allows a one-time boardroom presentation to live on in eternity online.

Notes

8

Communicating Through
E-Mail and E-Newsletters

E verybody seems to know what e-mail is, but many small business owners are not using it as wisely as they could, especially when it comes to communicating with potential customers. These e-mails need to contain some graphics within an attractive layout in order to get noticed and avoid a direct path to the trash or spam folder. Sending plain text e-mails to customers is considered "old school." Small business owners with limited resources need to ensure their electronic messages are received and (ideally) acted upon.

E-Mail Visibility

When an e-mail message arrives in a user's Inbox he immediately sees two key pieces of information about it: the sender's e-mail address and the subject. Most senders can figure out a catchy subject line when it comes to e-mail marketing, but some e-mail programs will truncate overly long subjects, so the recipient might see only the first part of it. The sender's e-mail address is important for a couple of reasons. First, the address is typically the first thing the recipient sees when scanning a long list of new messages in his Inbox. In an Inbox clogged with unsolicited messages, an unrecognizable e-mail address may not get a second look before being deleted. Second, spam filtering software may route an e-mail directly to the bulk mail folder, bypassing the Inbox all together.

Domain Names and E-Mail

If you've registered a custom domain name for use with a Web site (i.e., YourDomainName.com) it is essential that you apply that domain name to all e-mail addresses the business uses. "Sales@YourDomainName.com" is much more professional looking than "BusinessName@aol.com" or "MarySmith729@comcast.net." Practically speaking, if you use an e-mail associated with a custom domain name, you will never have to change e-mail addresses if you change Internet service providers (ISPs).

For example, an e-mail address ending in "@aol.com" is associated with an AOL account. As soon as that account is closed, the e-mail address dies with it. If that e-mail address is printed on business cards and other marketing materials, which then require updating, the change can represent quite an expense and hassle. With the domain name-based e-mail, the address does not have to change as long as the domain registration is current.

Domain name-based e-mail addresses are aliases in many cases. Alias e-mails are like 800 phone numbers: they serve to direct e-mails to a mailbox that is hidden from the sender. For example, if you send e-mail to CustomerCare@DanStone.com, that e-mail gets routed to a Yahoo! mailbox. There is no mailbox at CustomerCare@DanStone.com; it is only an alias that redirects the mail to the appropriate Yahoo! mailbox. Yahoo! offers several paid e-mail services that enable outgoing e-mail to have a custom domain name return address, thus hiding the Yahoo! e-mail address. The business owner gets all the benefits of the Yahoo! Mail service – online calendar, address book, and notepad, and an interface that closely resembles that of popular e-mail programs like Microsoft Outlook. The e-mail is then conveniently accessible from any computer or mobile device with an Internet connection.

Foiling the Spammers

A standard e-mail link on a Web site (often called a "mailto link," in reference to the HTML code associated with it) is an open invitation for spammers to grab that address for their evil doings. Instead of providing an e-mail address as a text link, create a graphic that contains text showing the e-mail address (see example on next page).

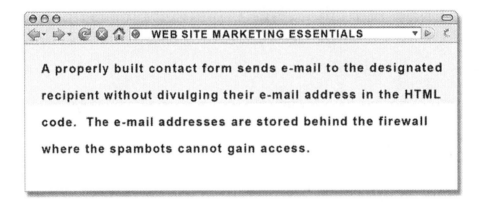

Button Containing E-mail Address

This graphic – readable by human eyeballs, but not spambots, since it is not plain text – can then link to a contact form on the Web site. The user can contact the business by filling out the contact form and clicking the "Submit" button, or he can manually type the e-mail address into a new e-mail message.

> **WEB SITE MARKETING ESSENTIALS**
>
> A properly built contact form sends e-mail to the designated recipient without divulging their e-mail address in the HTML code. The e-mail addresses are stored behind the firewall where the spambots cannot gain access.

(Please see additional discussion on contact forms, pages 84-85.)

Newsletters Via E-Mail

Sending regular e-newsletters to past and prospective customers is a great online marketing tool for small businesses, and the price is certainly right. Like a blog, an e-newsletter can provide useful, value-added information to recipients in addition to keeping them updated on services and products for sale. HTML-based e-newsletters allow a business to send an attractively formatted e-mail message complete with images and links. A handful of software applications allow anyone to build HTML e-newsletters on their own, but a better option is an online service that provides e-newsletter templates along with e-mail list management.

Constant Contact (see figure below) has emerged as the leader in Web-based e-newsletter creation and management services. Its service not only

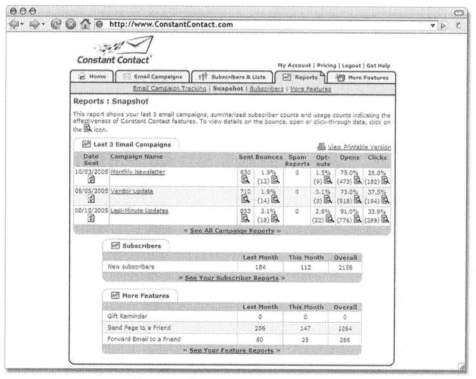

ContstantContact.com Reports Snapshot

includes the basics, (list management, graphical e-newsletter templates, and image storage), but also robust features like statistics that show bounced e-mails (the result of bad addresses) and number of recipients that click-through to the sender's Web site. Constant Contact offers a free trial to get started. After the trial period, pricing depends on the number of e-mail addresses in the owner's list.

Although it is possible to manage e-newsletter campaigns without paying a third-party provider like Constant Contact, many ISPs and other e-mail service providers limit the number of e-mail messages one can send per hour as an anti-spam measure. If you have an e-mail distribution list of 250 recipients and are limited to 25 outbound e-mails per hour, that's 10 hours to send out one newsletter.

9

Making Contact Pages Magnets
for Local Consumers

Most Web sites have a bland "contact us" page that provides the physical street address, an e-mail address, a phone number, and a link to a map on an external Web site. Those pieces of information should definitely be there, but making a few strategic additions can prove useful when it comes to helping local consumers find the site in the search engines.

Local Searching

More than one-third of searches performed in the major search engines include a geographic identifier as part of the search. Users frequently search for "pizza delivery 10012" instead of just "pizza." This is not only because users prefer placing online orders from stores close to them (faster delivery), but they are also looking for brick-and-mortar stores to patronize in person. (Please refer to Chapter 3's discussion on Google and Yahoo! local, page 39.)

Instead of simply listing the address on the contact page, include directions from various local communities to the business. For a retail store in Berkeley, Calif., for example, the Web site should have directions along these lines:

> From points north (I-80 southbound) – including the cities of Benicia, El Cerrito, Richmond, San Pablo, and Vallejo – take I-80 south to the University Avenue exit and head east…
>
> (Repeat for other cities in the surrounding area.)

This strategy adds geographic keywords (i.e., city names) to help capture local searchers' clicks. A similar approach is to list a dozen or so of the major zip codes the business serves, placing them at the bottom of the contact page. If someone is searching for "steak restaurant 68127," having both the zip code and the search terms together on one Web page is ideal.

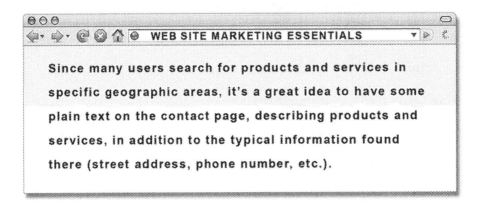

Since many users search for products and services in specific geographic areas, it's a great idea to have some plain text on the contact page, describing products and services, in addition to the typical information found there (street address, phone number, etc.).

Even just a few sentences of plain text describing the products can make a significant improvement in the contact page's search engine prowess.

Integrating Interactive Maps

It is possible to embed a live, interactive map from Google or Yahoo! right onto your contact page itself. Users can click, drag, zoom and even view satellite imagery without following a link off the site to Google or Yahoo! Maps. This is not only convenient for users, but also gives Web sites with the maps an interactive boost.

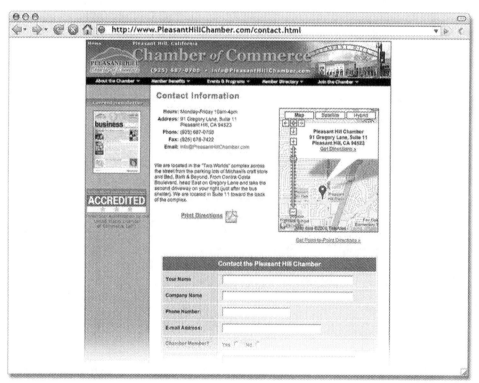

Pleasant Hill Chamber of Commerce Contact Page with Integrated Google Map

Incorporating a Google Map onto any Web site, for example, requires a free Google account and some cut-and-paste level HTML skills. See http://www.Google.com/apis/maps for more information.

Contact Forms

At a minimum, the contact page should have a simple form for users to fill in and send a basic inquiry to the business. The contact form offers the small business a great opportunity to learn something about prospective customers and capture their e-mail address for future e-newsletter mailings (with users' permission of course). The contact form should request the customer's name, address, e-mail address, and phone number, as well as other information that might help the small business owner:

- Have you shopped with us before?
- Are there goods/services you would like to see us sell?
- Are you a member of our organization?
- Would you like to receive a brochure?

How Contact Forms Work

Contact forms are processed by scripts – little programs that take what the user types in, packages it up, e-mails it to the designated recipient, and presents the user with a "thank you" page so he knows his message has been sent. Most Web site hosting companies provide their clients with scripts that are easy to implement. However, the scripts they provide are often vulnerable to spammers. Be sure to ask your Web developer to check whether the script stores the recipient's e-mail address or if the address gets written into the HTML code for the Web page. The latter will give spammers access to the e-mail address. You do *not* want to see something like this in the HTML code for the contact form:

```
<input type=hidden name=recipient value=you@yourdomain.com>
```

Another type of spam relating to contact forms comes from spambots filling out the contact form and submitting it. The spammer never needs the recipient's e-mail address; it just submits the equivalent of spam e-mail via the form, and the "form spam" is e-mailed to the recipient. The best way to deal with such spammers is to add a CAPTCHA (Completely Automated Public Turing Test to Tell Computers and Humans Apart) to the form. For more information on CAPTCHA see Wikipedia.org/wiki/Captcha.

Regardless of the form-processing method used, all scripts eventually get hacked by spammers. Script authors typically provide fixes that Web site developers must diligently install for their clients in order to keep their contact forms from becoming spam conduits.

Printer-Friendly Contact Information

Users frequently like to print out the contact page and map and take it with them en route to a location they haven't visited before. If the map is provided via a separate mapping Web site such as Yahoo! Maps, there is a good chance that it may not print as expected. Incorrect street names may creep in, newer streets may not show at all, or the user may be forced to print several versions of the map at differing zoom levels to get what he needs.

An easy solution that users really appreciate is to provide a printable version of the business' contact information along with a map at a printer-friendly resolution (e.g., 300 dpi) in Adobe PDF format. Not only is the Adobe PDF format reliable (it's been around for more than 10 years), but users have also come to expect PDF versions of information they would commonly print, such as forms, and publications like newsletters.

Click-to-Call

Phone numbers displayed on Web pages need to be compatible with mobile phone browsers. It's possible for Web developers to build HTML phone links, but most mobile devices will automatically recognize phone numbers as long as they are written with hyphens and not parentheses or dots between digits: use 408-555-1212 *not* (408) 555-1212 *and not* 408.555.1212.

10

Measuring Success with Web Site Statistics

The computers on which Web sites are stored (Web servers) log a variety of data that can help us understand how well a Web site is doing from a marketing standpoint. Stats show how users found a Web site (i.e., referring Web sites), the keywords they used in search engines that led them to the site, and the Web pages visited. For small business owners looking for basic information about their sites and visitors, the best Web stats tool available is from Google, at Google.com/analytics. Best of all, it's free!

Google Analytics presents both basic and detailed statistics visually in charts, graphs, and maps and well as numerically in tables (please see figure on next page).

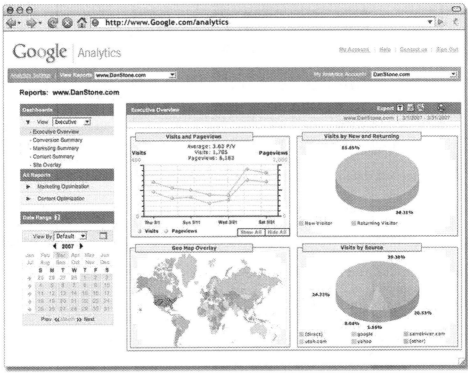

Sample Google Analytics Report

Enabling Google Analytics on a Web site is easy: it simply requires copying and pasting a hidden HTML code fragment on the bottom of each Web page of interest. One Analytics account can be used to track multiple Web sites, making it valuable for Web developers as well as business owners.

The advanced analysis tools Google Analytics offers are impressive and include a "Site Overlay" feature that shows clicks as a visual overlay on actual Web pages. "Funnel Visualization" shows pages where users first enter the Web site (it isn't always at the home page) and where they abandon ship. Looking at a particularly popular abandonment page might reveal problems with that page. Checking Web stats on a regular basis is important for the small business owner, especially after changes to the site are made.

Notes

11

Web Site Marketing Essentials Checklist

The preceding 10 chapters provide a number of suggestions for increasing the online visibility of Web sites and converting visitors into customers. Below are highlights for easy reference. This list can serve as a "to do list" for small business owners:

- ❏ **Examine your home page** in terms of its adherence to UHPF

- ❏ **Add or enhance plain text** especially on your home page

- ❏ **Check <TITLE> tags on all pages**

- ❏ **Check your site's link text** for opportunities to add keywords

- ❏ **Build a site map** and enhance it with additional text

- ❏ **Check how your domain name is being written** (use caps for words within it) and **consider registering a second domain name** with keywords in it (then **redirect** the shorter one to the longer one)

- ❏ **Research opportunities to get new external links to your site,** ideally with keyword-laden link text

- ❏ **Start a blog** and add at least two entries every month

- ❏ **Open a PayPal account** and sell at least one item, such as gift certificates, or perhaps develop a white paper or resource guide to sell for a few bucks

❏ **Register with an affiliate program** such as Amazon.com's

❏ **Add an interactive feature** if you don't already have at least one

❏ **Start collecting e-mail addresses from clients/customers** if you haven't done so already; open a free trial account at ContstantContact.com and send out an e-newsletter

❏ **Ensure that your outgoing e-mail messages appear to be sent from a custom domain name-based address**, such as You@YourDomain.com, not You@InternetServiceProvider.com

❏ **Enhance your contact page with additional city names,** zip codes, descriptive text, an integrated interactive map, and a printer-friendly version

❏ **Ensure phone numbers can be clicked and dialed on mobile devices**

❏ **Open a Google Analytics account** and add the tracking code to your Web pages, then review your Web stats after one month

Appendix

Screen Captures of Web Sites Employing the
Universal Home Page Formula

The Web sites presented on the following pages employ the Universal Home Page Formula with some variation (refer to Chapter 2). Small business owners can draw inspiration from these sites, benchmark desired features, and provide direction to their Web consultants, saving time and money on their own sites. Regardless of industry, as demonstrated by the eclectic range of home pages that follow, UHPF can be applied to maximize any Web site's appeal and effectiveness.

Many of the following sites do not heed the recommendations of this book when it comes to search engine optimization (see Chapter 3). These sites compensate for their lack of SEO efforts by extensive expenditures on other forms of advertising; expenditures that small business owners wouldn't normally be able to afford. Good Web developers should be able to create search engine-friendly sites using the designs and layouts shown as a guide.

Neither the author nor the publisher approves of or endorses any of the products or services described on these sites.

Andersen Windows

www.AndersenWindows.com

AT&T

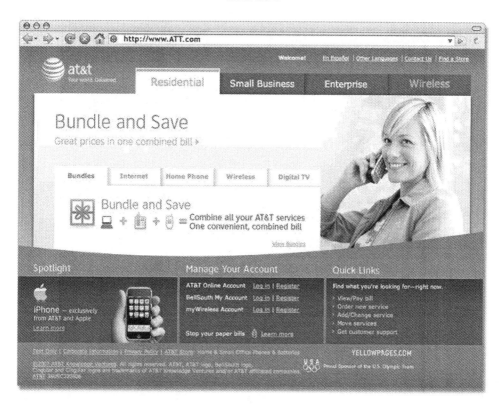

www.ATT.com

Columbia Sportswear

www.Columbia.com

Crate & Barrel

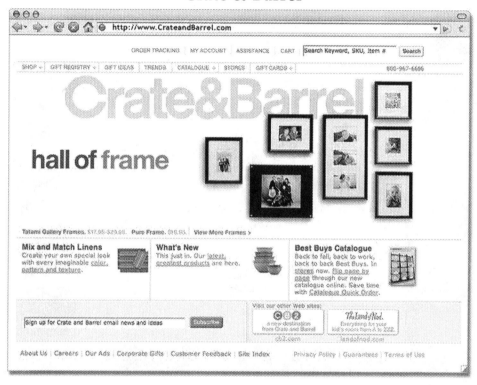

www.CrateandBarrel.com

Crutchfield

www.Crutchfield.com

Curaçao Tourist Board

www.Curacao.com

Dole

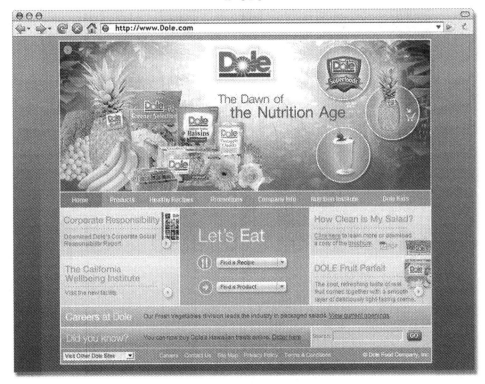

www.Dole.com

Griffin Technology

www.GriffinTechnology.com

Home Depot

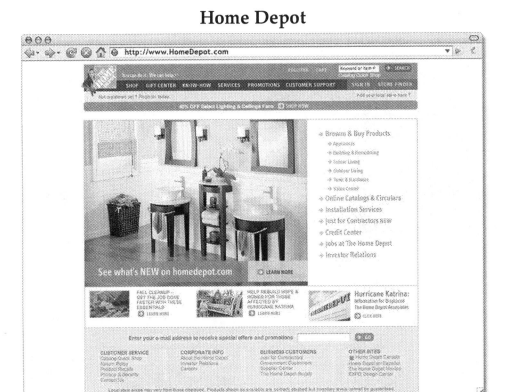

www.HomeDepot.com

Islands Restaurants

www.IslandsRestaurants.com

Jack in the Box

www.JackInTheBox.com

JetBlue Airways

www.JetBlue.com

Jiffy Lube

www.JiffyLube.com

Kensington

www.Kensington.com

Kohler

www.us.Kohler.com

Lexus

www.Lexus.com

.Mac

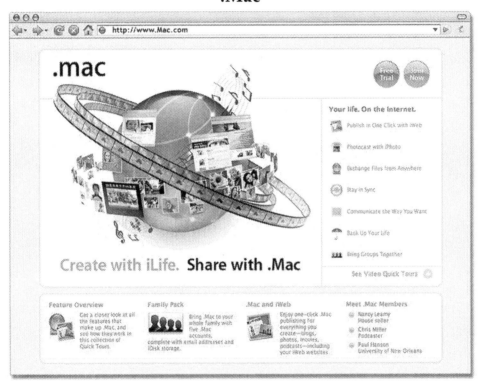

www.Mac.com

Maxtor Solutions

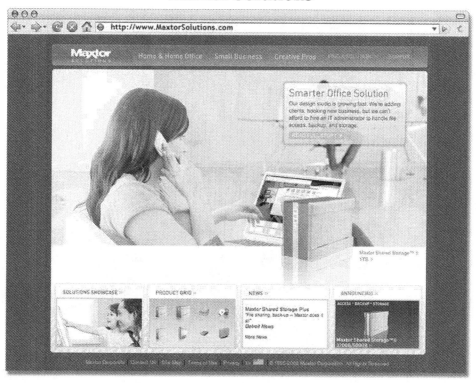

www.MaxtorSolutions.com

Monterey Bay Aquarium

www.MBAYAQ.org

Network Solutions

www.NetworkSolutions.com

Nike

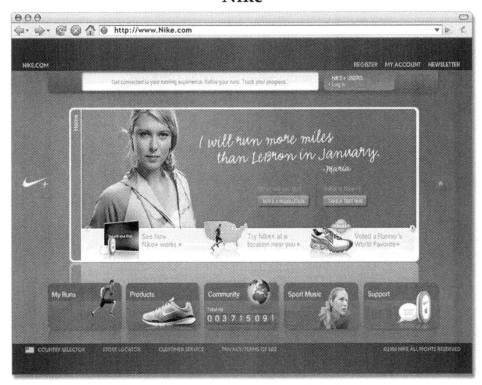

www.Nike.com

Nikon Digital

www.NikonDigital.com

Nissan USA

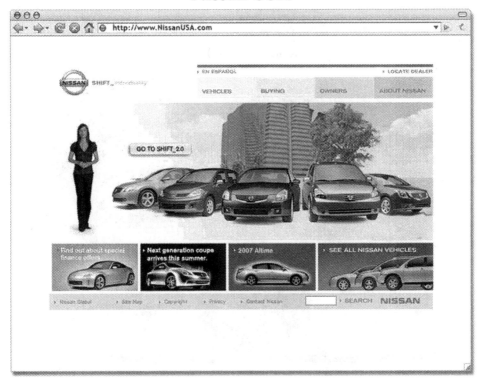

www.NissanUSA.com

Nokia 770

www.NokiaUSA.com

Opera

www.Opera.com

Pearle Vision

www.PearleVision.com

Peet's Coffee

www.Peets.com

Pepperidge Farm

www.PepperidgeFarm.com

Pier 1

www.Pier1.com

Pioneer Electronics

www.PioneerElectronics.com

Ruth's Chris Steakhouse

www.RuthsChris.com

Shutterfly

www.Shutterfly.com

Sonos

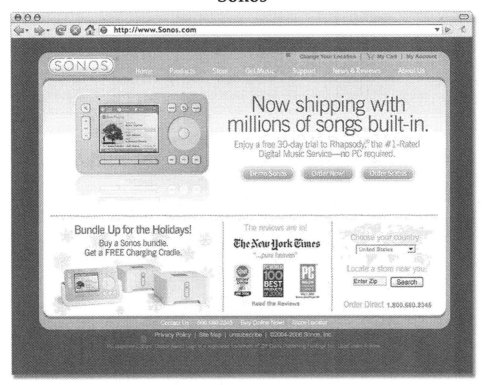

www.Sonos.com

Sony Classics

www.SonyClassics.com/whokilledtheelectriccar

Southwest Airlines

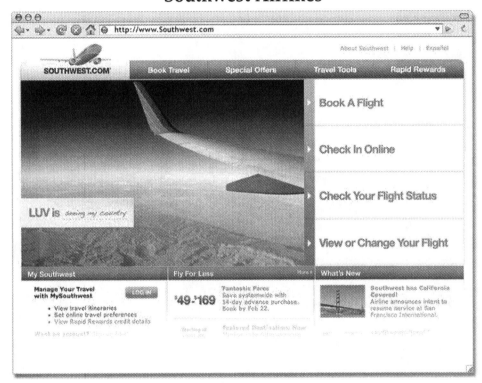

www.Southwest.com

Sun Microsystems

www.Sun.com

Target

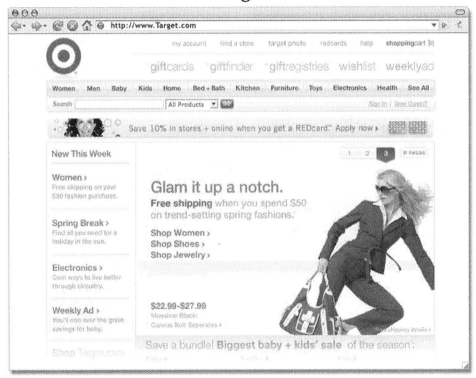

www.Target.com

Toto

www.Toto.com

Toyota

www.Toyota.com

Trek Bicycles

www.Trek.com

Verizon Residential

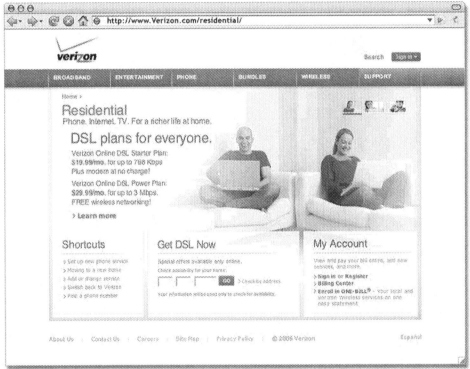

www.Verizon.com/residential

Vonage

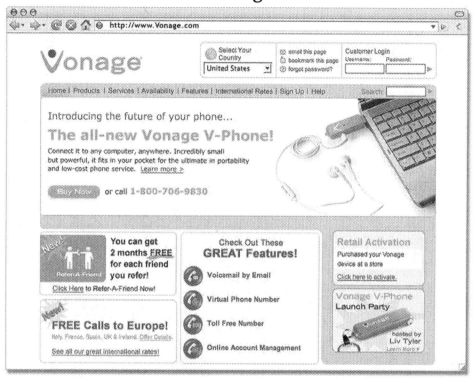

www.Vonage.com

Windows Vista

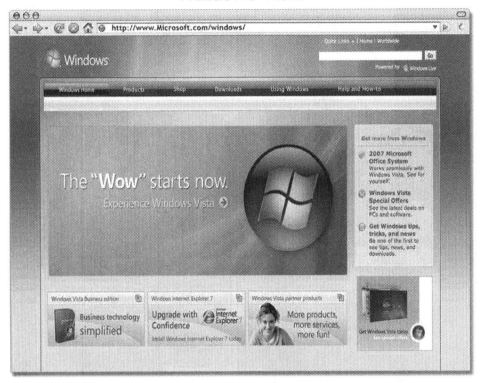

www.Microsoft.com/windows

XM Satellite Radio

www.XMradio.com

www.ingramcontent.com/pod-product-compliance
Lightning Source LLC
Chambersburg PA
CBHW080423060326
40689CB00019B/4352